5 STEPS TO DRAWING
AIRCRAFT

by Pamela Hall • illustrated by Jane Yamada

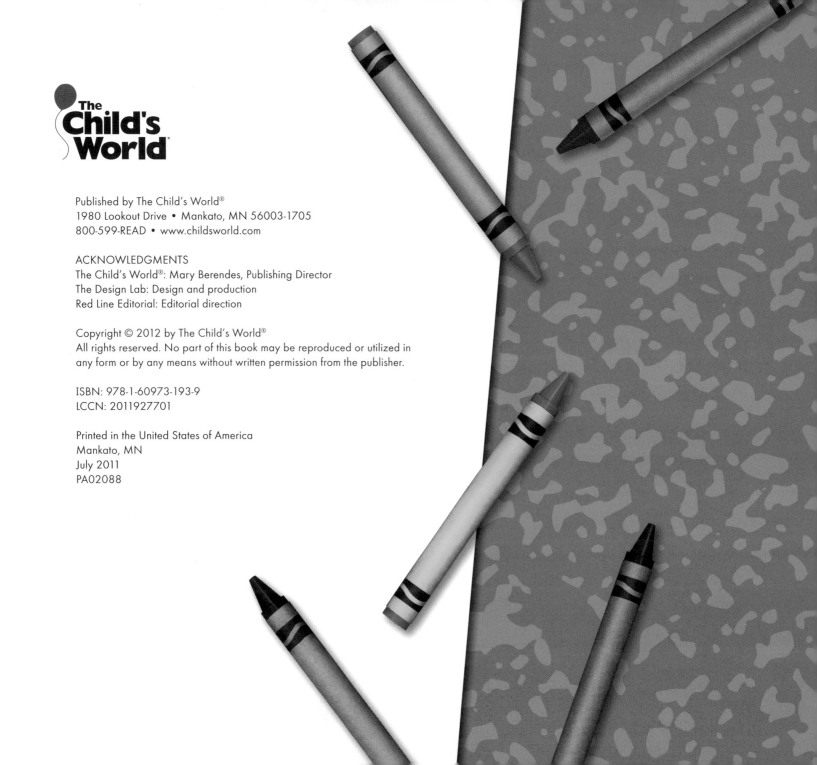

The Child's World

Published by The Child's World®
1980 Lookout Drive • Mankato, MN 56003-1705
800-599-READ • www.childsworld.com

ACKNOWLEDGMENTS
The Child's World®: Mary Berendes, Publishing Director
The Design Lab: Design and production
Red Line Editorial: Editorial direction

ISBN: 978-1-60973-193-9
LCCN: 2011927701

Printed in the United States of America
Mankato, MN
July 2011
PA02088

TABLE OF CONTENTS

THE DREAM OF FLYING

Early humans dreamed of flying. They looked to the birds. What was their secret of flight?

People tried flapping around in wings made of feathers. But their bodies were too heavy. They finally found a way to get their feet off the ground. They had to become lighter than air! In the 1700s, balloons and blimps began flying in the skies.

But humans still wondered: How do birds fly so fast and so high?

Their hollow bones help. So do strong muscles moving long, stiff feathers. Humans watched air flow above and below those feathers. Soon, they found how airplanes could get into the air with the right speed and other **forces**.

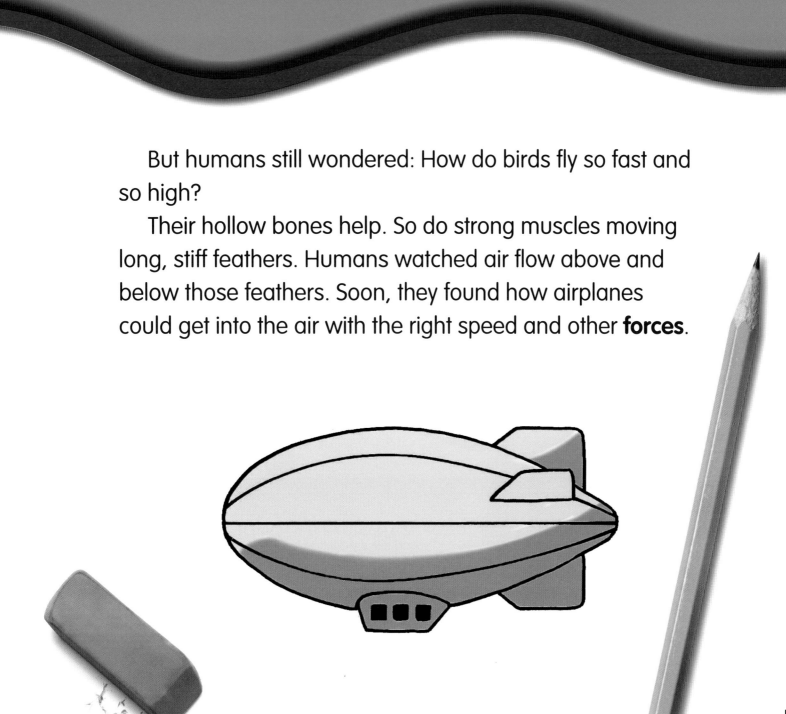

HISTORY OF FLIGHT

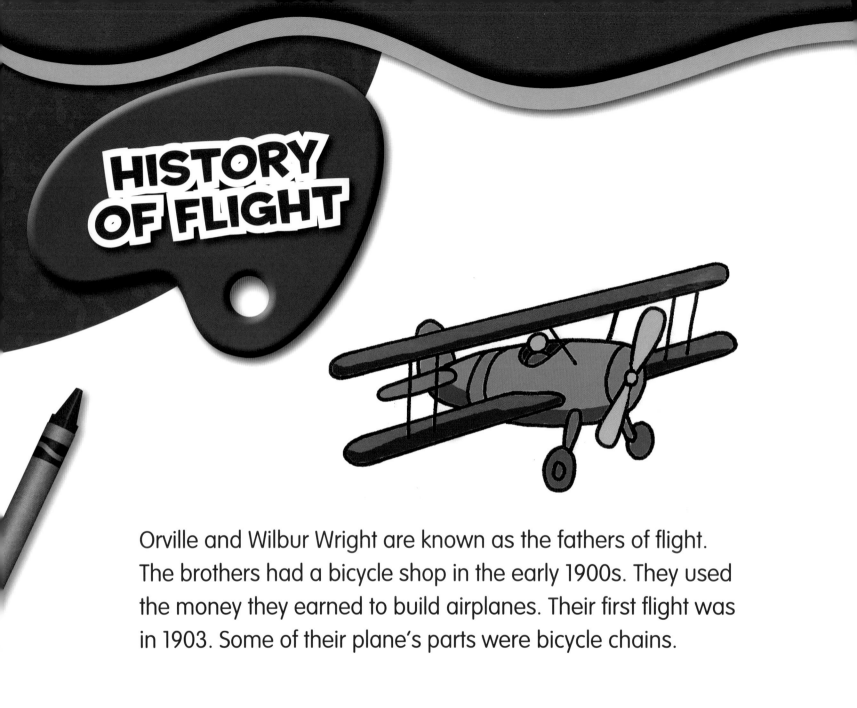

Orville and Wilbur Wright are known as the fathers of flight. The brothers had a bicycle shop in the early 1900s. They used the money they earned to build airplanes. Their first flight was in 1903. Some of their plane's parts were bicycle chains.

About ten years later, biplanes fought in World War I. Biplanes were early airplanes with two sets of wings. People kept finding ways to build better planes. Crowds gathered to watch **pilots** set records in speed, distance, and **altitude**.

Then, jet power changed the world of flight. It let jet liners fly longer distances. Jets were much faster, too. Most flights people take today are on jet liners.

FLYING TODAY

People use aircraft all the time. Jumbo jets take people to faraway places. Big cargo planes ship things we use every day. Helicopters help save people lost in thick forests. Fighter jets help out in wars.

Flying can be used for fun things, too. People fly kites and hang glide. They ride in hot air balloons to see as far as a bird.

Floating, gliding, and soaring. We have made our way into the sky. Most of these inventions happened in 100 years. What do you think will happen in the next 100 years?

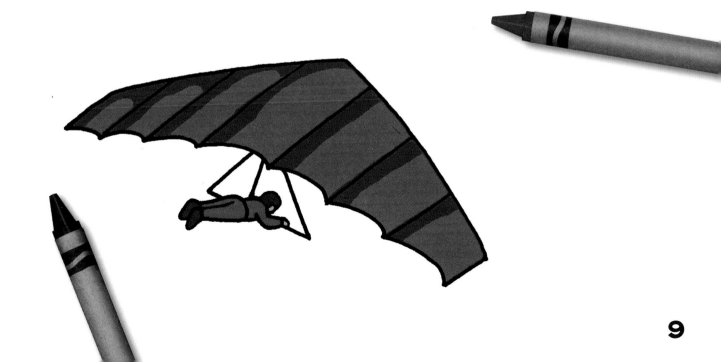

DRAWING TIPS

You've learned about aircraft. You're almost ready to draw them. But first, here are a few drawing tips:

Every artist needs tools. To learn how to draw aircraft, you will need:

- Some paper
- A pencil
- An eraser
- Markers, crayons, colored pencils, or watercolors (optional)

Anyone can learn to draw. You might think only some people can draw. That's not true. Everyone can learn to draw. It takes practice, though. The more you draw, the better you will be. With practice, you will become a true artist!

Everyone makes mistakes. This is okay! Mistakes help you learn. They help you know what not to do next time. Mistakes can even make your drawing more special. It's all right if you draw a plane's wings too big. Now you've got a one-of-a-kind drawing. You can erase a mistake you don't like, too. Then start again!

Stay loose. Relax your body before you begin. Hold your pencil lightly. Don't rest your wrist on the table. Instead, move your whole arm as you draw. This will help you make smooth lines. Press lightly on the paper when you draw or erase.

Drawing is fun! The most important thing about drawing is to have fun. Be creative. Your drawings don't have to look exactly like the pictures in this book. Try changing the size of the hot air balloon's basket or balloon. You can also use markers, crayons, colored pencils, or watercolors to bring your aircraft to life.

1

2

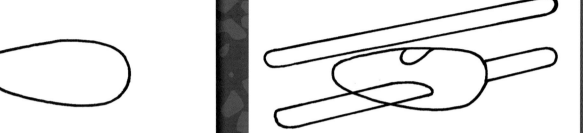

BIPLANE

3

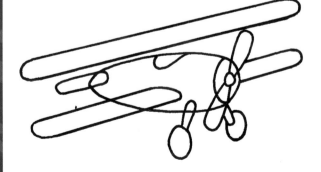

4

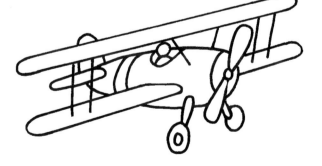

A biplane can twist and turn better than planes with just one set of wings. Fighter pilots rolled and spiraled high in the skies in biplanes.

5

1

2

JUMBO JET

3

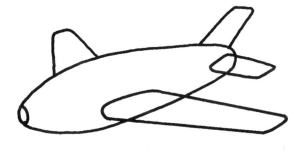

4

A jumbo jet is the largest type of aircraft. These jets carry hundreds of people at once. The blinking lights you see in the night sky are jets carrying people from one place to another.

5

1

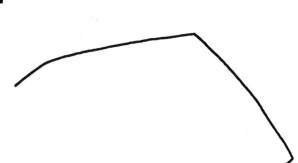

2

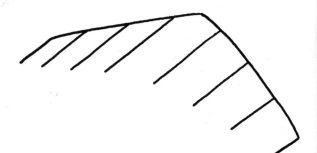

HANG GLIDER

3

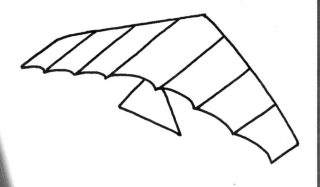

4

A flight on a hang glider starts out on a windy ridge high above the ground. The pilot jumps off. The pilot shifts his or her weight and moves the control bar. This steers the glider.

5

1

2

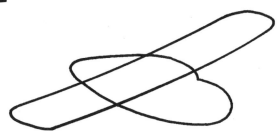

SEAPLANE

3

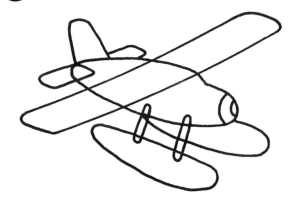

4

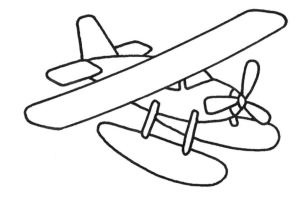

A seaplane takes off and lands on the water. It has floats underneath to keep it from sinking. These are the only parts that get wet.

1

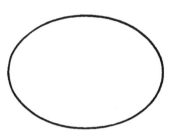

2

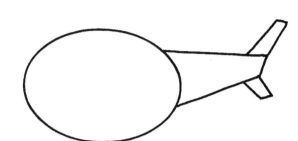

HELICOPTER

3

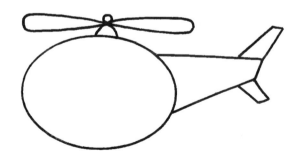

4

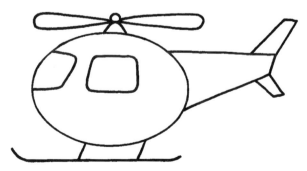

Helicopters don't need a runway. They have **propellers** on top to help them go straight up into the air. They can take off and land from just about anywhere!

5

1

2

FIGHTER JET

3

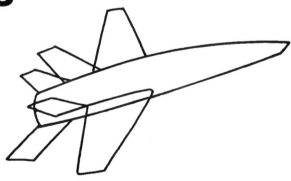

4

A fighter jet moves quietly and quickly. A pilot sits in a **cockpit** made of clear, strong plastic. He or she can see all around.

5

1

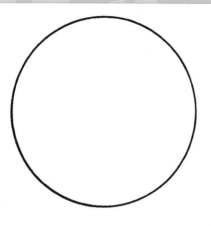

2

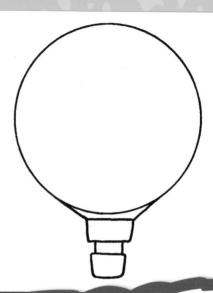

HOT AIR BALLOON

3

4

The wind mostly decides where a hot air balloon goes. But the driver controls altitude with the burner. Turning the burner on makes the balloon rise in the sky. Turning the burner off makes the balloon go down.

5

1

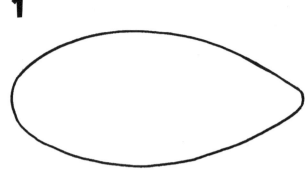

2

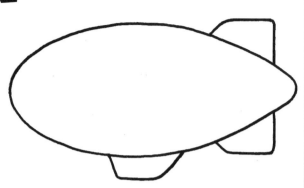

BLIMP

3

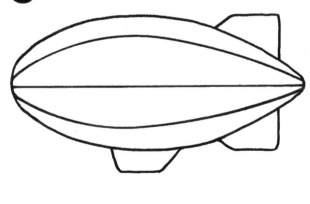

4

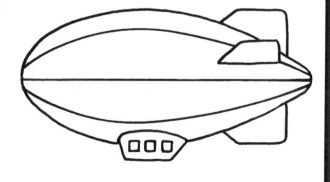

A blimp uses gas that is lighter than air to rise into the sky. A blimp moves forward like an airplane. It can hover like a helicopter, too.

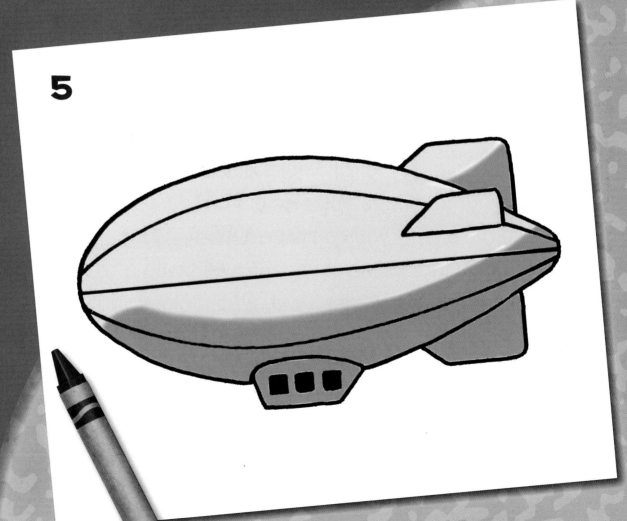

5

MORE DRAWING

Now you know how to draw aircraft. Here are some ways to keep drawing them.

Aircraft come in all different colors, shapes, and sizes. You can draw them all! Try using pens or colored pencils to draw and color in details. Experiment with crayons and markers to give your drawings different colors. You can also paint your drawings. Watercolors are easy to use. If you make a mistake, you can wipe it away with a damp cloth. Try tracing the outline of your drawing with a crayon or a marker. Then paint over it with watercolor. What happens?

Drawing Real Aircraft

When you want something new to draw, just look around. Have you ever seen an airplane flying in the sky? What did it look like? The next time you are at the airport, take a closer look out the window. Is the airplane big or small? Does it have a long row of windows or only a few? What color is it? Now try drawing it! If you need help drawing real airplanes, use the examples in this book to guide you.

GLOSSARY

altitude (AL-tih-tood): Altitude is the height of something above land or water. A plane can fly at a high altitude.

cockpit (KOK-pit): A cockpit is the control center of an airplane. A pilot sits in the cockpit of the airplane.

forces (FORSS-es): Forces are any actions that change the shapes or movements of objects. Several forces, like speed, are needed to make airplanes fly.

pilots (PY-luts): Pilots are the people who fly aircraft. Pilots have to train a lot to fly an airplane.

propellers (pruh-PEL-urs): Propellers are sets of rotating blades that move a vehicle. An aircraft's propellers help move it in the sky.

FIND OUT MORE

BOOKS

Emberley, Ed. *Ed Emberley's Drawing Book: Make a World*. New York: Little Brown, 2006.

Gravel, Elise. *Let's Draw and Doodle Together*. Maplewood, NJ: Blue Apple Books, 2010.

Shields, Amy. *Planes*. Washington DC: National Geographic, 2010.

WEB SITES

Visit our Web site for links about drawing aircraft:

childsworld.com/links

Note to Parents, Teachers, and Librarians: We routinely verify our Web links to make sure they are safe and active sites. So encourage your readers to check them out!

INDEX

ABOUT THE AUTHOR:
Pamela Hall lives near the
St. Croix River in Lakeland,
Minnesota, with her children
and dog. Along with writing
for children, Pamela enjoys
being outdoors.

ABOUT THE ILLUSTRATOR:
Jane Yamada began her career
in Los Angeles, California, doing
work for various ad agencies, toy
companies, and entertainment
groups. She now lives in Colorado
and illustrates children's books.
Most of her art is pen and ink
drawings with watercolor.